LET'S BRUSH OUR TEETH

By Sandie Muncaster

Art by Jovan Carl Segura

Library For All Ltd.

Library For All is an Australian not for profit organisation with a mission to make knowledge accessible to all via an innovative digital library solution. Visit us at www.libraryforall.org.au

Let's Brush Our Teeth

First published 2019

Published by Library For All Ltd
Email: info@libraryforall.org.au
URL: http://www.libraryforall.org.au

PNGAus Partnership

This book was produced by the Together For Education Partnership supported by the Australian Government through the Papua New Guinea-Australia Partnership.

Original illustrations by Jovan Carl Segura

Let's Brush Our Teeth
Muncaster, Sandie
ISBN: 978-1-925932-11-9

We have teeth.

Teeth are used to chew.
CHOMP CHOMP

Food makes our teeth dirty. Yuck!

Let's clean our teeth.

Clean teeth are strong.

You will need a toothbrush.

And toothpaste.

Open wide!

Brush your teeth.

BACK AND FORTH! UP AND DOWN! ALL AROUND!

Spit and rinse.

Now your teeth are
sparkly clean!

ABOUT THE AUTHOR

Library For All works with authors and illustrators from around the world to develop diverse, relevant, high quality stories for young readers. Visit libraryforall.org.au for the latest news on writers' workshop events, submission guidelines and other creative opportunities.